JOHN FRYE

2016

A Simplified Financial Retirement Plan

Keep it simple

This book describes a very simple and
solid process for a secure financial
retirement plan.

Acknowledgements:

"A Simplified Financial Retirement Plan" is my fourth book in four years, and I have to say, it has been a blast. I have really enjoyed writing these books.

I would like to thank my wife, Sue, for her help with the editing of the first draft of this book. I thank my entire family and all of my friends for their continuous support of my writing projects. I would also like to thank Kerri Bennett for helping with the final edits and formatting of this book.

Contents

Introduction 3

Chapter 1: Getting Started 8

Chapter 2: In the Beginning..................................13

Chapter 3: The Education 21

Chapter 4: The Next Step 30

Chapter 5: Points to Ponder and Review.............46

Chapter 6: Putting it all Together 56

Chapter 7: Investment Strategy 66

Chapter 8: The Investment Setup..........................72

Chapter 9: Death and Taxes 87

Chapter 10: Help is Available.................................90

Chapter 11: Summary..102

Introduction

Making money and putting it to work can be a fun process, if done the proper way with the right attitude. It will give us financial freedom. The best thing about this plan is: this can be done at almost any income level.

Building a secure financial future isn't something one can do overnight. It will take some time, and it will take a lot of work. But I truly believe that anyone can achieve this. Everyone needs a plan. It doesn't just happen. However, we can make it somewhat easier with the right plan. We need to make this plan fun and profitable. Do not have your life be identified as – saved too little, borrowed too much.

"Happiness lies not in the mere possession of money. It lies in the joy of achievement, in the thrill of creative effort." – Franklin Delano Roosevelt.

A Simplified Financial Retirement Plan

Retirement planning is complicated for many of all age groups. In the early years, many put off saving because they think retirement is eons away. Then, in their 40's and 50',s these folks panic and race, trying to catch up.

We'd all figure out how to do it, and we'd create a capacity within our lifestyle to save, first of all, but also have a spending rate that's living below our means. It really all starts with an effective budget plan.

Simply put, you can save less and finish with more if you get started early in life and harness the power of compounded investment returns.

The power of that early contributor who lets his or her money compound over time is a really really important message to understand. I say save early and save often.

Retirement is not just about money, but it sure helps to have enough to enjoy your later years in life. A happy retirement is planned. Our life can be viewed in three stages:

- In the first stage, our parents and teachers tell us what to do.
- In the second stage, our employers give us directions, usually within set working hours.

- In the third stage, when we retire, what we do with our time and lives is something we must each decide. In this stage, we are still creating our lives. Life is certainly not over by any means. This stage of life is not simply about looking back. Retirement is a transition to a new beginning, but what you have done previously will have a great deal to do with what you do next. We are still creating memories.

We are our memories, including the unhappy ones. We learn from our previous experiences, even our failures. We do not want our lives in this new age to be a repetition of previous failures but a life of wisdom and satisfaction. We are still writing our story, and the question now is, "Where do I want to go next in this story of my life?" None of us knows how long that story will be, but it doesn't hurt to plan for the longest time possible, keeping in mind the possibility of declining health or income in the later years. Thus, there is a need for "The Simplified Financial Retirement Plan".

The transition into retirement, with seemingly endless options, can be very challenging to say the least.

The information that I am sharing in this book has helped me to gain some financial success. I do not take any responsibility for actions taken by any of my readers. This is just a pattern that I found to be successful for me. Everyone needs to perform a self-evaluation as you plan for your retirement. I can only hope some of my ideas may help you along the way.

Good luck!

If you have read any of my other books, you know that I began my journey of life with very little money (no money, actually). I was trying just to survive the moment with no thoughts of retirement. In book one "The Turns in Life", I related my early family life and growing up and attending high school in rural Arkansas.

The second book covered the rest of my life, "The Turns in Life – After High School." The third book covers my 50-year career in the paper bag industry, "The Multiwall Matrix."

All of my books are available online at www.amazon.com. You may purchase them as an e-book or a paperback. You can also contact me at johnnyfrye@sbcglobal.net, and I will mail you a signed copy.

Now, this current book will tell some of the interesting and exciting events along the way as I tried to become somewhat financially secure enough to retire. Some are good and some not so good. You work hard for your money. You have to work even harder at keeping it. I hope you enjoy this book.

Chapter 1: Getting Started

As one begins to focus on your financial freedom, you will want to have money to invest in order to build long-term wealth. There are essentially two ways to generate more money: You can make more, or you can spend less. Pretty amazing, right? It all boils down to that.

The universal lament about money is that there is never enough.

John D. Rockefeller, the founder of Standard Oil and once the richest man in the world, was asked how much money was enough.

He answered, "Just a little bit more."

In my opinion, he was correct with this answer. Wealth cannot satisfy, but it can make living much easier, if it is managed wisely. Diligent planning is a cornerstone for successfully managing personal finances.

Here's another potential surprise: In a lot of cases, it's actually easier and more "profitable" to get more money by spending less than it is to always worry about making more. Why? Because when you make more, you pay 25 to 35 percent in taxes on that extra income. If you generate money by spending less, 100 percent of that savings will immediately drop down to your bottom line.

Spending less doesn't mean that you have to pinch pennies to the point of taking all the fun out of life. I believe that this mistaken notion is what drives people away from saving in the first place. In fact, you need to control your spending only to the point of ensuring that you can pay yourself in a savings account and still meet your other obligations. The alternatives aren't very attractive. If you can't save, and instead go into debt, you will quickly find yourself in financial trouble.

Therefore, don't kid yourself about savings. If you have $10,000 in your savings account, and you have $10,000 in debt, you have no savings. And in my opinion, it is actually even worse than that because interest rates on the credit often run from 18 to 21 percent. If you are making less than that on your savings, you have what I call reverse leverage (not a good thing). Reverse leverage compounds you into a financial grave, and you may not even see it coming until it is too late.

Again, spending wisely does not mean that you have to be a miser. Instead, you should review all areas of your life and learn how to reduce your spending comfortably.

One should constantly be in the habit of spotting potential saving opportunities. Many times, these may be small savings; however, these will mount up to something big later on. This is especially true if we use these savings in conjunction with compound interest.

Some still believe in the American Dream, and, therefore, they are willing to work incredibly hard to make it come true. Their faith is well placed. In fact, wealth can still be made in America today but only if you establish the right financial goals for yourself and are willing to work hard to achieve them.

Millions of Americans today fail on both counts. They don't set realistic goals, and they don't work hard at achieving financial freedom. Many waste money on lottery tickets and "get rich quick" schemes. Despite the odds against success, and despite the fact that even for the winners, these kinds of financial windfalls rarely lead to lasting financial success.

There is no greater truth than this – money makes money. It likes clustering together. It breeds quietly and quickly. The rich get richer and the poorer get poorer.

When you have some money, you'll be astonished at how fast it can grow. I recommend you understand and learn the concept of compound interest as quickly as you can. If you spend all that you make, the compound interest theory will not work for you. You have to have some money for this to work.

I think that most everyone these days has money of some sort. You chose what to do with it. You can set a standard of living within that means and live from paycheck to paycheck, or you can elect to take a portion of your money and make it grow into something much larger than you could ever expect. It just takes a little planning and investing along life's way.

If you follow the basic principles outlined in this book, you should be able to have and enjoy the things that you want, no matter what your income may be. There is no magic bullet to a get-rich-quick scheme. For me, the elegance of this book is its simplicity and practicality. Our world has grown so large and complex that we are often overwhelmed by all of the technology and media bombarding us.

If you leave your money in a low interest-bearing checking account or savings account, you will not get there. Inflation will eat your lunch, so to speak. You must create a good solid base and then take some educated risks in order to reach your goal.

No matter how you measure "rich," success in attaining your definition of wealth comes from two basic factors – managing your financial life with a budget and keeping a tight rein on consumer debt.

The endless flood of often-misleading financial offerings, from credit products to untenable mortgages, has set off an unprecedented wave of financial disaster for naïve consumers. I can't tell you how important it is for all of us to remember that we are now living in a world of "Borrower Beware".

It is up to each of us to take charge of our financial lives. We must take our decisions about income, purchases, savings, and investments seriously.

Chapter 2: In the Beginning

In order to get things started in the right direction, one needs to start saving for retirement as early as possible. This makes this process so much easier. Believe it or not, you can take this "Simplified Financial Retirement Plan" and get started at any phase of your life.

Start NOW!

Sorry, I didn't mean to yell. I just got a bit too excited, I guess. There is no more important step than getting started, now.

The longer you put off saving and investing, the harder it will be to build enough of a nest egg to make life easier in the future. Investing is a long-term process by which you build wealth, and it has two basic components – saving and compounding. Saving is the act of putting money away for the purpose of investing. Compounding is what money does for you by earning interest. Together, these two processes grow your money.

When you think of the foremost attributes that determine long-run success in investing, does a graduate degree in business come to mind? Holding a coveted title at a top investment bank? Being a successful entrepreneur? I hope not. In my opinion, if you thought "Yes" to any of these things, then you were 100 percent wrong!

I believe that the primary attribute that guarantees successful investing is time. Period. End of story! It's fortunate that young people may have more of this precious time than any other. Therefore, I urge everyone to get into the game and start acquiring wealth. All of us have the potential to be wealthy; we just need to rethink our dollars and cents.

The fabulous thing about investing is that your money can compound on top of itself over and over again. Also, the longer your investment horizon, the better you can deal with risk. We will cover more about this compounding strategy later in the book, so continue on.

You have to have a plan. If you don't have a plan, you'll be tempted to fritter your cash away, spend it instead of investing. If you have a plan, you will know exactly what does and does not fit into it.

Before you can control your finances, you have to stop the leaks. You may have enough money, but it leaks away before you get to spend it in a whole variety of ways – taxation, paying interest, lack of use (not invested properly), or too much being spent on the wrong things. Before you can control your finances, you have to stop the leaks.

Keep a record of everything that you spend over a period of time to see where all of your money is going. This data will be very helpful with your "Simplified Financial Retirement Plan".

It is fine to have a credit card, but you need to pay it off in full every month in order to avoid the high interest rates. If you do this, you will be in a strong, forward-going position with your financial plan.

The key is to build a bit of capital and invest it wisely. By all means, use an investment professional, but don't be used by them. Most of them try very hard, but in the end, most of them fail to grow money any faster than the market index.

Once you decide to follow this "Simplified Financial Retirement Plan" or any plan, you will need to put some money aside until you have a modest reserve fund built up for emergencies. Once this is in place, set up an IRA or 401(k) and fund it aggressively, starting as soon as possible.

Do not show off by buying expensive, high-status possessions or consuming leisure in a way that projects a lifestyle you can't afford.

Don't expect that you have the right to live luxuriously as you enter middle age and beyond. People can only afford to live as well as their finances allow—not as well as they feel life entitles them to live. Do not play games with your finances. You must face reality and live in the real world.

You may say that you wish that you had started saving and investing sooner. This would certainly been a great idea, for time is money, especially when you join the saving and investment world.

However, never dwell on the past. Instead, focus your energy on the future, for that is all that you have some control over. Simply make the best of the situation. You can learn that a small amount of money saved and invested can turn into a large sum over time, if you have a "Simplified Financial Retirement Plan".

Don't swing for the fences with your investments, for risk and reward are joined at the hip. Use low-expense index funds to broadly diversify your holdings so that you get returns that commensurate with the amount of risk you're taking. I will cover much more on this subject as we continue.

As I wrote in my previous book, somewhere late in my career, I reviewed the possibility of starting my own business. My job as a plant superintendent of a large paper bag operations ended when I was 58 years old. I began to search for ways to continue my own consulting company offering technical, safety, and quality management services.

About this time, another large paper bag operations offered me a full time position as a packaging engineer. This job certainly fit me to a tee, since I had so much experience in this field. I would be doing exactly what I like to do.

I am currently employed as a full time packaging engineer, and this allows me to further my career and not have the hassle involved with self-employment.

What a deal! It works for me. I am now very near retirement (2016).

In 1944:

I was born on November 16, 1944 into a very poor family. I had three brothers and a sister. I was the baby of the family by nine years. My father passed away when I was ten years old. My youngest older brother, Bill, took over as the head of our household, which at that time was only Bill, my mother, and me.

Bill was only 19 years old at the time, but he stepped up to the challenge and made a living for us while I remained in school. We were able to qualify for welfare help, even though we really did not want to accept this help. This made us feel kind of shameful. My limited family really wanted to make it on our own. But a few years after my dad passed away and mother became ill, we were forced to rely on this help. Even though the help was very small, it kept us from going hungry. We received $20 per month and a once a month trip to the commodity barn, where we were given powdered milk, corn meal, and cheese. However, small these items were, they were very much appreciated at the time. I was the only person in my immediate family to have the opportunity to graduate from high school.

As I have stated many times in my previous writings, we were very poor. My family had always been poor; therefore, we knew nothing else. We just learned to make the best of it and be somewhat satisfied in our own little family world.

I really didn't have a chance to make much out of my life. There was no desire to do anything but to find a way to barely get by financially. I don't think we even knew what the word "financially" meant back then.

There was no money, therefore no bank account. This meant that we didn't have to worry about saving or balancing a checking account. My family worked on a farm and received pay for the days that they worked. We only made enough money to barely get by. We spent our money on the bare necessities as far as it would go, and then we would do without until we earned a little more money. We accepted this as a way of life back then.

When I graduated high school, I had no money, and my family was still barely getting by. I studied very hard and finished high school with a 3.00 grade point average.

I also received a few college scholarships, but I did not attend college. The year after I graduated from high school, Bill got married, and it fell as my lot to take care of my mother. This, I did for several years. We moved to Pine Bluff, AR and rented an apartment. Mother and I lived there for a couple of years, and then I married my wife, Sue. My mother lived with us for a couple of years after that. Thank you, Sue for your help with her. I know it wasn't an easy chore. But, we made the best of it.

Chapter 3: The Education

It is a shame that you have to learn the financial story on your own by trial and error experiences. There is not nearly enough taught in high school about how to handle finances. I guess they are too consumed in trying to give you an education to earn a decent living to get caught up in the fanfare of showing you how to be able to take care of what you earn.

I think there is a large void when it comes to teaching a young person about finances. In the early years, most high school graduates could not even balance a checking account at the end of the month. As a matter of fact, back then, I think it is safe to say that most people in my circle of friends didn't even have a checking account.

I think that most young people think that old age is something that happens to other people, but that they will live fast, die young, and have a beautiful corpse. The last thing they want to hear is that one day they'll be like their parents or grandparents.

Your first goal should be to increase your human capital by getting a solid education and developing excellent work habits, making connections, and cultivating a pleasant personality. I think life is like the old saying: You are what you eat. Also, to take this a little farther: You become much like the ones that you associate with.

Most people in the '50s and '60s lived from paycheck to paycheck. There was so little money coming in that they couldn't enjoy much more than the very necessities of life. And as time moved on, it was very difficult to get kick started in the financial world because there was a need to obtain so many things just to feel that one was able to even think about a savings account or an investment account.

I think most people thought that even if they lived long enough to retire that by some miracle they could make ends meet financially until death. In the early years, the Social Security payment was so small that one could only hope that if they lived long enough to draw this money, that this, along with Medicare and

Welfare, may kick in so they could at least survive in retirement.

When the United States enacted Social Security in 1935, allowing people to receive a government pension at age 65, the average male life span was 62 years. President Roosevelt, who initiated the legislation for Social Security, died at the age of 63, and his primary staff aide died at 55. It was an accomplishment to make it past age 65 in those days. Today, the average life expectancy is over 80.

Where retirement once signaled an ending to active life and a move to the rocking chair (or recliner), and then the hospital bed, and then death, today it is the start of a whole new phase of life. This stretch of 20 to 40 years of probably healthy living is unprecedented in human history. People used to work right up to the time of death. The new norm is to live into what was once considered "very old age," with many of us living until age 90 or 100.

All of this brings our question, and point of this book, front and center, "What will we do with that period of time?" When can I retire financially? We are in the frontier of a whole new age of living.

A Simplified Financial Retirement Plan

I know from experience that my family had no thought about any retirement plan. I guess they just stuck their head in the sand and just blocked out the thought of ever retiring. They would just do the retirement thing like they did everyday life. That is, just live life from day to day and not worry too much about tomorrow, let alone have any thought about retirement.

Early in my life, I learned to be conservative with my money. It was just too hard to earn to just blow it on things and entertainment. I had to have more for my hard work. I would imagine how difficult it was to earn a buck. If I were going to spend $25 on something that I really didn't need, I would ask myself if I really wanted to spend the money that it had taken me several days to earn. Most of the time, my answer was no.

I learned early on what a dollar was worth in my world. And now I am so glad that I developed a good savings and investment attitude.

As we continue with this plan, I must repeat that this is only an outline of a simplified financial plan that worked well for me. It has been very rewarding, fun, and exciting for me to see my net worth grow from month to month and from year to year. I hope that someone can gain some knowledge of how important it is to get an early start on saving and investing for retirement and being able to become financially secure at an early age.

Of course, as all of the financial advisors will tell you that the past investment cannot guarantee anything for the future. However, past data can give all of us some much-needed information to help us make some good solid investments.

Even though now the times have changed so much, I really don't think the past data can really reflect much on our future. You just need to focus on the happenings around you today and make the best decisions that one can about saving and investing for the future. For who knows what the future will bring? If it continues to change as fast and as much as it has in the last few years, we may not be able to recognize it.

What we could all use – adults and young people alike – is a major dose of financial education, and trust me, I'll get up on my soapbox about the need for a widespread literacy effort in this country throughout this book. It just kills me that so many of our children get absolutely no financial guidance from their parents or the schools. I hope that you will share this book with your kids – or better yet, give the book to them to read as well.

In this book you will find the basic question: How much money do I really have to spend? It is amazing to me that very few people have any idea how much they can spend before running into trouble. That is because of the ease of using credit cards that seem to never have a good ending.

To me, the more money you have to spend, the less you have to worry about paying the bills and stressing out over every penny. But there is more to it than that. A big paycheck isn't necessarily the catalyst for contentment. The real source of happiness is having control over your money and knowing that you have more coming in than going out.

After I learned how to make money grow, I really enjoyed seeing this happen. It is very difficult to break into the comfortable saving and investment system when you have nothing to begin with. But, I did it, and I will explain the system that has been very success for me.

As I began to work in my life-long career of paper bag making, there was no money in my life. The bag-making career has been very good to be. It afforded me a decent salary, and I believe I received a salary increase each and every year. The salary was very small in the beginning. The first year I received a .02

pay increase. This wasn't very much, but I was making a good salary for my location. There were only a few jobs around that paid much more.

When you have nothing to begin with, it is very difficult to even think about saving any money. The need to just get by is greater than any savings plan could be. There are so many things that one needs to just get up to par:

- An automobile
- A house
- Furniture for that house
- Insurance

Then there are the things that one wants. All of this takes real money to purchase. I have to say, at the time of my growing up into manhood, the credit card era was a lifesaver. I was able to get up and going by utilizing credit card purchases. I just had to be really careful and keep those purchases under control. One could purchase needed items and only pay a small amount of money on these purchases per month; however, the interest charges on the purchases were rather high.

Despite it all, I think everyone needs a credit card to use in this world today, but you need to be really careful with how you use it. You will need this card to rent a vehicle. You can use it for emergency funds, also. Just be sure to pay it off monthly or ASAP to avoid the high finance charges.

You have to be really careful in the management of a credit card. There is nothing more corrosive to your financial health than leaving a balance on your credit card. If you're only paying the minimum payment due each month, then you are really in trouble.

It's imperative that you live within your means. And borrowing on credit cards isn't part of that scenario.

I have to say that I was able to get kick-started in my financial career by utilizing credit. In the early years, there was not enough money to pay cash for any of the large items needed to move up in life.

I guess my early struggles in life with money allowed me to be more aware of how important it was to learn to handle my finances. It took many years of hard work just to get to the point that I could even consider saving anything for retirement or such.

There was also something in the back of my mind that always came to the forefront—I needed to put aside some of my earnings for a rainy day.

At work, I remember, I got my savings plan kick started when our credit union came into being. I just signed a note allowing the credit union to withhold some money from each of my paychecks to be placed in a savings account. This was so easy even though it was only $5/week.

At least I was saving and this made me feel really good. After a while, it got really tempting to take this savings account and buy something that I really wanted and probably needed at the time. And I did this on more occasions than I should have. Anyway, I was on my way to becoming financial secure, someday.

Chapter 4: The Next Step

Early on, when this credit union savings account began to grow, I met this wonderful girl, Linda Sue Porter, and the love of my life. We were married January 27, 1967.

Of course, this gave a whole new meaning to saving money for retirement. I now had to buy a house and everything that goes into this purchase. My wife and I started with almost nothing between us, and now we have reached the retirement years. We had another chore in our lives to help us spend some of our savings. This was our precious son, Jonathan. He was born on July 11, 1974. He was the best thing that ever happened in our lives. He is now married to Shannon Beckwith Frye, and they have a couple of children, a daughter, Jillian Kate; and a son, Joshua Caleb. They are my very precious grandkids. I didn't know it at the time, but I think I must have been saving for them right along with retirement.

I cannot think of a better way to spend my money than on my son and his family. I could have retired early in life, but I have elected to continue to work because I enjoy working. When I turned 66, I really thought about retiring, but I could now receive my full Social Security pay out and continue to work and make a full salary. They told me that they didn't care how much money I earned; they were still going to send me a check every month. There was a little catch to this process, for I would have to pay federal income taxes on 85% of my Social Security payment. Now, how fair is that? I think I have already paid taxes on this money, once.

My wife can also draw ½ of my Social Security payout, even though she has not paid into Social Security enough to draw anything on herself. Also, as I continue to work, my Social Security payout grows every year along with my wife's. I now will have much more to save and invest. I really do enjoy working, saving, and investing. It is so much fun finding new ways to save money and then search out the very best investments going and then watch it grow. What a deal!

Also, be aware—Many say that if you continue to work after you turn 66, do not draw the Social Security payout. You just need to let it grow about 8%/year and then draw this money when you turn 70 years old, and your monthly check will be much greater for the rest of your life.

I say draw every penny of Social Security that you can at the age of 66 and invest it because if you die before you reach 70, no one will ever receive a penny of your Social Security money that you paid in over all of your working years. Of course, you will not need this if you are dead. How true? But your survivors will not get it either.

If you plan on leaving an inheritance, I say take the full retirement amount pay out at 66. The Federal Government has looked at the data history, and is playing the odds game with your life. That is that you will die in their time zone, and they will not have to pay out any of your Social Security that you paid in to them over your hard working years. I don't think this is a fair game. But who said that there are very many fair games in life after all?

I think the real plan for Social Security was to help the unfortunate to have financial relief if they ever needed it. Of course, that got out of hand fairly quickly, since no one can figure out who the unfortunate ones are any more. So everyone gets Social Security, whether you need it or not. Therefore, the costs have skyrocketed.

I can remember, several years ago even, when the Social Security withholding was very small, the annual payroll deduction was met well before the end of the year. Now the costs are very high and going higher each year.

Now they say that the Social Security account is going broke. They are paying out more than they are taking in. Now how can that be, since we have elected the very smart people to be in charge of all of these issues? Isn't this about the same thing that I have been writing about—Spending more than you are making?

Now, that is where we are now, so let me explain the road that I traveled, financially to get here.

The plan in the beginning was to live a good modest life and enjoy it along the way. Sue and I had most everything that we wanted and a little extra every once in a while. The paper bag-making occupation paid me a nice salary with annual pay increases and many promotions along the way. Of course, with every promotion, came a pay increase.

33

Note that at each pay increase is a great time to think about an increase in savings or investments because this is new money that you didn't have. I only hope that you have not already spent the increase before you get it. Without some planning, this can happen. So be aware, please save about ½ of all pay increases. You will be glad you did in the later years.

I could have changed jobs several times and received even more pay increases. Of course, this would have meant family relocations each time. So, I elected to stay with the same company for most of my working career. This has been a very good and very successful decision for me.

If we take this "Simplified Financial Retirement Plan" in steps as we go along, the first step was the Credit Union weekly savings plan. It began to grow, for we did not take any money from this plan unless there was an emergency. I guess you could stay this had become our "emergency fund."

I didn't know this at the time, but most all financial advisors say, first, that one needs to set aside money for emergency needs. As the world turns, there will be difficulties. Bad and unexpected things happen. We need to be prepared for these emergencies. Do not panic. Just keep your head up, and use the emergency fund to provide the money to get you through the crisis. Even during this time of need, you need to pay really close attention to your spending. It may seem like everything is going against you, but persevere. You can survive.

This emergency fund allows us to concentrate on your real savings plan as we move along.

In the early years, this credit union savings account was very small, but as I received pay increases, I increased the automatic withholding a little bit each time. This helped me secure more money than I had ever had in my lifetime, which wasn't much, since I had started out with no money.

About this time, Sue and I had been saved and were living a Christian life. We joined a local Freewill Baptist Church. Now, this was a giant step in our lives. We began to do what God asked all Christians to do, and that is to give back a portion of that which He has allowed us to have. I think without a doubt that this decision to give back has helped me secure more than I could have ever imagined of having. Thank you, Lord!

The second early step in the "Simplified Financial Retirement Plan" was a purchase of some church bonds. Our local church decided to build a gymnasium and additional Sunday school classrooms. This building project was financed with a 15-year bond program. Bonds could be purchased in $500 or $1000 increments. These bonds paid 10% dividends. During this time, dividend and interest was at a very high level and you could get very good rates on certificates of deposit (CDs), or Treasury notes. I didn't know anything about these or any other investment strategy at this time.

However, I had learned very much about giving back to the Lord and how He blesses one for this giving. Therefore, I invested as much as I could at this time in these church building bonds. I took ½ of my savings to invest in these bonds. That was $10,000. With a 10% dividend, the principal doubled every 7½ years. Therefore, in 15 years, this $10,000 investment was $40,000. What a deal! Now here we go on deep into the "Simplified Financial Retirement Plan".

This is where I learned a lot about compound interest. In my opinion, compound interest is the key to building wealth. Simply put, it means investing some money, earning interest on your investment, and then leaving both the interest and the principal in place so that you can begin to earn interest on your interest (as well as on your principal). This is hard to say or write, for it gets you a little tongue-tied.

In other words, first, your original money earns money, and then the money your money has earned earns more money. This goes on year after year. After years of compounded growth, the annual earnings reach an acceptable level. Eventually, if your original investment is large enough, if your rates of interest were competitive, and if you wait long enough, your nest egg will grow large enough to produce an acceptable outside income. Sounds simple enough, right? A safe almost no fail plan. Not so fast. Even though this is a great plan, and one will be wise to follow this compound interest system with the major part of one's investment, there are many other fun ways to make money and watch it grow. Then, as you accumulate more money, it just makes sense to place much of it in the compound interest system.

My next step was the 401(k) Plan at work. This was a great plan, for my employer matched up to 5% of my savings into this plan. I began the plan by placing 8% of my salary into it. What a deal! Now we were getting somewhere. This 401(k) account began to grow by leaps and bounds. This money was before taxes, so that gave me even more money to add to my credit union savings account.

My job began to offer a company stock plan. This was an easy savings plan, but I knew it was risky. At this time, my company seemed to be plenty sound, but I didn't want to take a chance that the company may take a dive for the worse, and I would not only lose my job, but also most of my investment savings. Therefore, I kept this investment on the small scale. I enrolled by having $5/week withheld from my paycheck. The company then took this money, and as it accumulated, they would purchase shares of company stock with it. This was a great program.

About this same time, the company offered the U.S. Savings Bond Program. I also enrolled into this program. I also enrolled with $5/week withholding going into this program. At this time, when my savings into this program reached $50, they would purchase a $100 U.S. Savings Bond. That seemed like a really good deal. The catch was that I had to hold this bond until it reached its maturity date, which at that time was nearly 6-years. That was fine, since I was moving into a long-term financial system. Now I was getting diversified. I didn't have much money, but I was looking pretty good.

Now, on with looking for other ways of not only spending less money and still living a very modest life style, but also looking for more investment opportunities. By the way, this had become a lot of fun for me. It was exciting, and I was really enjoying this. I was finally getting somewhere with my life, and it had become very stable financially.

I have always tried to stay very conservative with the base of my money so that I can sleep better at night. And, also, I have always felt that my money was much too difficult to acquire to take very much risk and lose it all.

Therefore, you will see from this plan: The core of my finances will always be in a very conservative investment. However, as we move on deeper into this book, I will write more about taking some risk with a conservative amount of the retirement monies.

I found that it would be very difficult to become financially secure by being really conservative. I just wanted to make sure that I never lost everything; therefore, this plan has a very conservative base.

But now it is time to move on to some managed risks.

A Simplified Financial Retirement Plan

Investing is the next step in wealth building after you've established a good solid base with a savings account. The aim of investing, at its core, is simple: to earn profits by putting your capital at risk.

In a savings account, you are taking almost no risk. The money you deposit is pretty much guaranteed. The money you invest outside of savings is money you specifically want to put at risk in hopes of earning returns dramatically greater than you'll earn on your savings. It may not be there when you need it, or the value of your original capital might be sharply reduced. With investing, the only guarantee is that there is no guarantee.

But no guarantee is no reason to avoid investing and, instead, stash all of your money in savings. If nothing else, investing serves one useful purpose: It can give your nest egg an opportunity to outpace the ravages of inflation.

Every year, for the most part, living your life grows increasingly more expensive. Interest rates on savings accounts and money market accounts—the safe investments– do not keep up with inflation. Thus, your dollars in those accounts are actually losing in value. That is a hard concept to accept. But that is life, and it doesn't look as if that is going to change anytime soon.

But, now that we understand this as a given, let's move on.

Once the savings plan gets some real ground roots, it is time to take some risks in the stock market. Over time, the data has proven that it continues to move on an upward tract. I would never suggest that anyone take everything and invest it into the stock market, although over time, this may have been the best place for all of your money. No way!! We will always keep our base saving and retirement money in place. We will only take risks with the extra money.

The stock market is a tricky story in itself. For instance, if you invest $1000 and it loses 50%, it is now worth $500. Now that $500 will have to gain 100% to get back to the original $1000. What kind of math is that?

I would have to say that I have earned a very nice return on real estate. I have owned three houses in my lifetime, and I have made a nice return on investment on the first two. I still have the third with a lot of equity in it, also.

The first house I bought with no down payment and a 30-year loan, for I didn't have any money. I kept this house for 25 years and sold it for about three times what I paid for it. The second house, I bought with no down payment and a 15-year loan. I kept this house for 13-years and sold it for about twice what I paid for it.

I bought my third house with several thousands of dollars down in order to eliminate the title insurance costs. I then financed the remainder on a 30-year loan. Now this was smart, since I had the money to do this. But wait, was it?

You can look at this several ways. One, you can take the tax advantage by deducting the interest charges off your income taxes or you can take a lump sum and pay the house off; therefore, you will be successful with the American dream of owning your own home. That is just what I have done.

Or you can take the extra cash and invest it into the stock market, which over time has had a better return on investment than the cost of the interest of making the monthly house payments. As I look back on this decision, it may have been better to continue with the 30-year loan and invest the cash into the stock market.

What do they say? Hindsight is 20/20 vision. I am very comfortable with my decision. I have a house that is paid for and a nice looking retirement portfolio. It is just human nature to always want more and to question your decisions. That is why I have written this book to give my readers some insight to a very realistic financial achievement.

In order to qualify this plan, I will say that by utilizing this plan over the last 20-years, I have been able to increase my net worth by a little over 12% per year. Now that is just not bad.

I started several years ago with nearly nothing, and now I am near retirement, and I am at a comfort level with this plan. It has worked very well for me.

Of course, the S&P 500 (stock market) fund has increased at an average of about 12% over this same time period. You say I would have been better off just to put everything into this fund? No. That was not for me. I must stay diversified. I will never place all of my eggs into one basket. History may repeat itself, but not with my money! You don't take that chance, for average is not good enough for me. So let's diversify.

Anyway, this comparison is not apples to apples because if I had my money invested in the S&P, it would have been tied up and not useful. My 12% average net worth included the use of my money, not only by heavy investments, but it also included buying stuff such as houses, automobiles, etc. Just using it to create a very good livelihood for my family and me. In most cases, my investments have averaged much more than 12% annually. Thus, here comes the creation of "The Simplified Financial Retirement Plan".

I have written about having an emergency fund. That is true, and one also needs a base retirement fund in place before taking very many risks. This will allow you to be more at ease with a great "Simplified Financial Retirement Plan".

It seems that in every life comes the need to get rich quick. Never, ever speculate with money that you have some better use for or that you know that you will need. Never put money down on anything illiquid if there's even a remote chance that you'll need to get your cash out in a hurry.

We all want to get rich quick, but for most people, that wish only leads to sorrow. You must know that the money you put up for these schemes has only a remote likelihood of making you wealthy, but it has a very real possibility of making you poor if you invest too much of it.

Some people don't believe in hard work, saving, and investing, being more interested in finding the right gimmick to make them rich. I don't say that no one ever succeeded in such endeavors; I only know that it hasn't happened to me, and I predict that it won't happen to you.

Chapter 5: Points to Ponder and Review

- Many Americans stand on the sidelines forever, missing out on the greatest builder of wealth available to the average citizen. Many Americans just never save or invest anything. In my opinion, this a huge mistake when it comes to retirement savings. No matter what your age, the best time to start saving and investing for retirement is now.

- Another big mistake is waiting too long to get started on saving or investing for retirement. The earlier you get started, the easier it becomes, especially when it comes to one of the best investment tools that I know. That is the use of compound interest.

- The odds are stacked against us at an early age, when we are just starting out, unless we have rich parents or have been given a large inheritance. Free money is a different story. You may not have anything left by the time you reach retirement, since you didn't have to work and invest long the way. It seems to me that the harder the money is to get, the more likely one will be to save and invest it wisely.

- Many Americans begin their professional careers saddled with credit card debt and student loans while trying to pay for all that life entails, often on a small starting-wage, just as I did. If you read my first book (The Turns in Life) or my second book (The Turns in Life-After High School), you have found that I certainly had nothing in the beginning. Both of these books are available on amazon.com.

- Investing in the stock market can be a lot of fun, if you are very careful, and you can make some real money. But be careful. Never invest the money that you need to make ends meet from day to day. I only started investing in the stock market after I had found that I could live within my means, and that is utilizing 70% of my income. All of my investments were very conservative in the beginning, mostly in the credit union savings. There I had a small amount of each paycheck automatically withheld and placed in a money market account. This account never paid much interest, but it was secure, and it was growing. The total interest on all of this money was only a couple hundred dollars each year. Not much, but it was something to let me rest at night.

- After I accumulated a good-sized nest egg, it seemed to me that I could take this nest egg and divide it up to secure 70% of that and take a slight risk with the other 30%.

- What a bright idea this turned out to be. This was the key to my financial success.

- Despite having more responsibility for their future financial well-being, the amount of investment illiteracy is frightening. Most people have not been taught how to manage money, and they are not willing to take the time necessary to do a good job managing their assets.

- Most people devote more time to deciding what to do on a Friday night than they devote to planning their asset allocation and the security selections of their investments.

- Putting together an appropriate investment portfolio is not brain surgery. Anyone can learn how to allocate their assets. The knowledge gained can be applied throughout your lifetime and passed down to the next generation. All you need is the desire to learn about investments and a little bit of time. The potential payoff is well worth the investment.

- Investment is never a one-time event; it's a lifelong process that requires fine-tuning.

- Always remember that your money is too important to invest without a plan. Everyone will have different needs and life goals; but you must have a plan, and that plan must be generated by an individual's circumstances.

- The sooner one starts investing and saving, the better. In the early years of one's life, the investments and saving may more than likely be small, so there will be very little money left over from the paycheck for any savings or investments.

- You should never put all of your eggs into one basket. You must diversify in order to distribute the risk. Diversification is not a panacea. It does not guarantee a positive total return over a particular time period. But diversification will spread out your risk, so maybe you can rest a little better at night.

- Market timing or knowing when the absolute perfect time to invest in or sell an asset is impossible. No one knows for sure what the market will bring tomorrow. An investment strategy solely focused on timing the market is an exercise in foolish guessing. You may win the lottery, but probably not.

- Yes, you can make a lot of money by investing heavily into a growing market, but with the large market swings, it is my conservative nature to stay with my 12% average net worth gain.

- A great way to buy stocks is to allow the dividends to stay directly in the investment. This is called a direct reinvestment plan (DRIP). I like to call it compound interest, and I am really fond of using in this process.

- The biggest risk of investing is doing nothing at all.

- The great hockey player Wayne Gretzky once said the key to being a successful hockey player is not knowing where the puck is but where it will be. The same logic applies to your money. In the investment world, asset allocation is the process that takes your assets from where they are now to where they should be in the future.

- After reaching retirement most financial planners will tell you that you should look to draw down your accounts at the rate of 4% per year. I think that my plan will allow me to take out less or maybe none at all. Wouldn't that be a great plan!

- When you retire the very best plan is to generate enough money from your investment to more than offset your withdrawals. If this is accomplished, a steady stream of income will be generated, and your principal can continue to grow.

- Withdrawals should take place from your nontaxable accounts before taking money from your taxable accounts. This way, your money in 401(k) plans and tradition IRAs continues to grow, tax deferred.

- It is very important to watch your expenses and live within your means. By the way, this is a great plan for your entire life. If you use this method, saving and investing will be a lot of fun, and your life style will be great. You do not have to live a like a hermit and try to save every penny.

- Live life to its fullest every day and enjoy what you have earned. Give to the church, save 30% for retirement, and live a great life on the rest.

- Then take 30% of the savings and investments and move up to a greater risk factor. Don't invest foolishly. Do a lot of homework and be smart about taking very much of a risk and it will pay off.

- After all, when you get to the point that you can get to a great and fun life on 70% of your income, then you can afford to take more risk on 30% of your savings. This plan allows you to rest better at night, for if the worst-case scenario happened, and you lost the entire 30% of the higher risk investment, then you would still be upset, but part of your retirement portfolio would still be fine.

- Therefore, gain all the knowledge that you can about investing and be as smart as you can, and everything will be fine. Remember you can lose some, and you can gain more from higher risk investments. Just be smart about it and do not panic.

- The longer you can hold on to an investment, the more chance there is that the long term growth in returns will overcome the short-term ups and downs in performance. The ability to hold an investment long term helps you tolerate more volatile investments and take advantage of the higher return potential they provide.

- Taxes are, unfortunately, another cost for investors. As the saying goes, "There are two guarantees in life: death and taxes." You may not be able to avoid them, but you want to defer them as long as possible.

- You need to try and hold securities with gains more than one year. This will give you what they call long-term capital gains. Anything sold before one year is called short-term capital gains. The taxes on long-term capital gains are much less than the taxes on short-term gains.

- Any psychologist will tell that along with death and public speaking, money matter always rank as one of peoples' biggest fears. Many worry about being able to afford to feed and clothe their families and provide them with safe places to live. We all know that these necessities do not come cheap.

- In handling their money, individuals make lots of foolish mistakes. Often errors get compounded into more errors, creating undue hardships.

- To create and ensure wealth for yourself and your loved ones, it is important for you to educate yourself and learn as much as you can about money and investing. There is never a downside to gaining knowledge.

- Saving all you can for retirement is not fun. It can be a burden. However, planning for retirement can be fun as you invest and watch your money grow.

- After all is said and done, if you do not believe in saving or investing for retirement, this still is a great plan. If you can live on 70% of your income, life will be a lot more stress-free. You can take the other 30% and have fun for a while or better yet, pay off some of your 70% bills, and then you will have more money for entertainment and stuff. But, be aware, if you live long enough, retirement will come sooner than you think. So, good luck with that plan and have fun!

Chapter 6: Putting it all Together

As I have said, this financial planning stuff is not taught enough in high school. I guess we are just supposed to learn it the hard way, by trial and error. This is dangerous to our financial lives because the error part will devastate us if we are not careful.

Saving and investing can be fun and very meaningful if there is a smart plan from the very beginning. It can be done later in life or anytime you become enlightened to the fact that the world is not going to hand you your financial life on a silver platter. It takes a lot of hard work and discipline to get a good financial plan started.

After all, when that first paycheck starts to come in, it feels so good to have some money of your own, and you really want to take it out and spend it. After all, you earned it.

But, wait a minute. Not so fast! The earlier you get started, the better it will be in the long run. You should start to think about investments and asset allocation when you first receive a paycheck. I really think this training needs to start in the home and carry over into high school. You really should not even wait for your first "real" job after you have completed your education. The first time you get paid for doing anything is the perfect time to consider what you are going to do with your earnings. You should save and invest part of your earnings, even if is only a small amount of money.

Kids are horrified to see how much taxes are taken out of their paychecks. Early on, part-time work can demonstrate firsthand what kind of work you may want to do for the rest of your life. If not, it may eliminate some work that you really do not want to concentrate on during your working years.

By starting young, you are also getting a head start on your savings. The chances you can take and the investing options available to you are generally much higher the earlier you start putting your money in the financial markets. Furthermore, by starting at an early age, you will be learning about investing. Textbook learning is helpful in investing, but it is no substitute for the knowledge learned from actually doing it. Experience is the best teacher. While you are young, there is time to make up for any mistakes you make and the opportunity to learn from your financial mishaps and correct them in the future.

If you take a step back and try to understand what your goals are for your assets, the picture can become much clearer. Block out the day-to-day noise and focus on the longer-term picture. Investing is a marathon, not a sprint. Slow and steady usually wins the race.

Low earnings and high expenses usually characterize the early stage, when you begin working full-time. The majority of people are single at this point and have some debt. It is very important at this early stage to think about saving and investing because good habits start young and form a foundation for a lifetime. Furthermore, by starting young, the power of compounding really works in your favor.

There are some simple ways to get started saving and investing. To become a major saver and investor, you have to figure out where your money is going. Therefore, track all of your spending. You may be surprised how much you can really save. Like I said a while back, the more that you can save by doing without, the more it will boost your savings, and that boost will be a lot more than a raise in salary because of the tax consequences.

Money management is really important. It is not glamorous, but managing money leads to most of the great things in life. The daily, ordinary details of life are what sets our financial futures. So we start *budgeting*.

Budgeting in the present and during retirement is a cornerstone of retirement planning. I think that living on a budget is like living on a diet. If you boil the best diets down to their essence, you get the same point: The way to lose weight is to eat fewer calories than you burn. To fix this imbalance, either eat less or burn more. It's just that simple.

The same goes for your personal finances. You simply spend less than you earn.

I think everyone should live on a budget...no matter how much money you have. Financial emergencies happen. A budget can help you prepare for unexpected large expenses. A budget can help us sleep much better at night, knowing that we have at least some part of our lives—our financial lives—in order. A budget allows us to manage our money and does not allow our money to manage us.

When setting up a budget, be certain to add in all of your annual expenses, and do not let them take a toll on your savings and investment account. For instance, take all of the bills such as annual dues, insurance, personal property taxes, etc. and total all of these bills and divide the total by 12 to get the monthly cost to be added to your budget expense as a monthly item. You will be glad you did this since, you will not get bind-sided into thinking that you are saving more than you really are.

Building wealth or reversing your downward spiral takes a lot of thought and planning. That's because so many forces work hard to compel you to spend your money rather than to save it. On the other hand, when you save money, equally powerful forces can operate to have your money work for you rather than for others.

Early in life credit is almost certain unless you have parents with no debt and a lot of money that will help you get started in your financial career. Most don't have this luxury, or the parents simply do not want to use their money to help their children get started. I think it may be a better learning and lasting experience if you do this thing on you own.

Now that you are putting at least ½ of all bonuses and raises into your retirement or investment account, you are very grounded in a great retirement plan. You certainly will be glad you did this later on. This compounding factor really kicks in with this long-term plan.

If you work for a company that offers a retirement plan, that is great, but by all means, do not count on this to make you rich when you retire. If your company offers a 401(k) plan, I say get in now! It doesn't matter how much you start contributing early on, just get into the plan, now.

Most companies that offer the 401K plan will match up to a certain percent or dollar amount. This is a no-brainer as far as I am concerned because if you will contribute the matching dollar amount, you have free money. Now, how easy is that? Wherever you feel comfortable starting with this plan, just get in, now!

If you receive an annual pay raise each year, be sure to raise your 401(k) contribution likewise. You will be glad that you did this, for this money, along with the compound interest, will grow rather rapidly. This will be one of the best investment tools to enhance your retirement.

Also, the 401(k) plan may have several investment options for you to direct your money. Especially in the beginning until you become a more advanced investor, please invest into the more stable investments. Do not put all of the money into any one account. You may want to be really conservative, and place it all into the stable or money market account. However, I do not suggest using this strategy long-term. The standard cost of living will eat away at your dividends and interest. A real caution here is do not place a large amount of your 401(k) contribution into you company's stock, if it is offered. You may think that your company is doing great and will always be around. I am here to tell you from experience that is not always the case. If you do not know much about investing, it would be wise to place your contributions into a balanced account. This is where the account is invested into many funds, and a couple times a year, it rebalances so that no one fund gets out of control. I kind of like this kind of fund. It is sort of like an index fund, which we will discuss later on.

If you have a few years before retirement, you can take more risks because you will have time for the economy to recoup. Also, remember, the investing plan is to buy low and sell high. One would be rich, if we could only figure out how to accomplish this feat.

One of the best ways to invest is by using the dollar cost averaging system. That is to buy now and buy on a regular basis over a long period of time. There are two ways to view the dollar cost averaging system. Over time, the economy will go up, and you will have more money, and then it will go down and you can buy more shares; therefore, when it goes back up, you will have even more money. The trick is to outsmart the market by staying put and not panicking and selling low, for - THIS IS ALWAYS A MISTAKE!

No matter how much money is coming into your household, you should make a very conscious effort to see that your expenses are always less. It is very important to try to make this spread between your income and your expenses as large as possible. How you handle your money is a lot more important than how you earn it.

Even though when you are young and just starting out it may seem like retirement is a long way off and it may be, it will slip up on you very quickly, and if you are not careful, you will not be prepared. So, pay attention!

So, you get through high school, and you need a car. Then here comes college – expenses, expenses, expenses. Then you meet someone you cannot live the rest of your life without. You finish college, hopefully, and get a job. You start earning a paycheck. Then here comes the marriage. Now you need a place to stay. Maybe, you can afford an apartment. Even though both of you are working, now here come the kids, and the wife may not work for a while afterwards, and even if she does, there will be daycare expenses. Welcome to the real world.

Now, you say, "How can I save or invest any money?" Where there is a will, there is a way. And you need to find it. If you are very disciplined and live below your means, you will find that way. It will be tough getting through the early years, but believe you me, it will be worth it in the long run.

You say, "I will just put my saving and investment plan on hold until I can afford it." This is not the correct game plan. For, if you follow this plan, you might never get back on track. If you are not tough enough to stick to living on 70% of your income, at least cut back some and keep the original plan intact. Do not get completely off track. It is just too difficult to get back on the right track.

It is very clear that everyone has some required expenses. I do not advocate sleeping on the street or going on a hunger strike to lower your bills. You should just be aware of your expenses, and try to reduce them where it is prudent. In many cases, tough choices and sacrifices are going to have to be made. Not getting the premium cable package, reducing the number of minutes on your cell phone plan, and bringing your lunch to work can take a bite out of your monthly bills over time. Saving a few dollars each day compounds into quite a bit of money over time. Try this saving plan, and after you understand that saving and investing can be fun instead of a burden, you will really feel good about yourself. It's OK to splurge a little every now and then, but just keep it under control, and you will be happy. After all, you will now be in charge and control of your finances. What a great feeling that is!!!

Chapter 7: Investment Strategy

I like to think that I made my money the "old fashioned way". I earned it! I did, most of it. The other money came from some simple investment strategies that I am about to share with you.

It doesn't matter how much money you earn, for if you have to state your lifestyle with your earnings, you will never get ahead of the money game. You will just be trying to stay up with the "Joneses". You do not have to look around very much to find many people with less than you have. So, there you have it. They must be living on less than you are. So why not join them and live on less?

One does not have to start out with the very best and the most expensive items to become successful. Just be patient, and you will get there soon enough. Guess what? When you reach that point, you may see that you really didn't want the very best things that life could offer anyway. Other things such as friendship, relationships, giving to the needy, etc. may just be on the top of your list.

I have never been an outgoing type person. I guess you could say that I have an introverted personality. I do not push very hard or demand much from anyone. I would rather do a job myself than expect too much from anyone else. I have found a way to make this personality work very well for me.

This has hurt me sometimes along life's highway, but I have found a way to get my own way, most of the time. I do not get too excited when I do not get my way quickly. I sometimes have to redirect my energy, but I will eventually get there. We need to challenge ourselves every day to be a better person and go out of our way to make others happy. Go that extra mile— it will make our lives much better, and we will have more fun in our lives. Try it; you may like it.

I use my ninth grade science class lesson here, also. Just like I do when I have a problem to solve. First, state the problem, and then look at two or three possible solutions, and get to work to make one of them happen. You will be surprised how easy this is.

First thing's first. Start out with a budget. This will help you keep your retirement goals on track. Don't think of it as a spending "diet" but a way to positively shape your financial future. Start out by tracking your cash flow, and then make adjustments in spending and saving that will pay off down the road.

In order to make this work, you need to list all of your expenses for a year. You can mark some money for extras or entertainment; just make it very small in the beginning. Next, add up all of your earnings and subtract your budget from these earnings.

Now that you see that you are spending more than you are making, welcome to the real world. You are like most everyone else. Changing this may take some work. However, do not give up. There is hope.

Rework the budget slightly, if possible. Cut your expenses everywhere it makes sense to do so. Just be careful not to cut out any necessities. You can do it!

The next thing is to make sure you live within that budget as much as possible. Congratulations! You are now on track. "What," you say. "This is still impossible. No way this will work." Hold on. It will work, so read on.

Next, continue on the budget, and as extra money is available, you must allocate most of this to your needed emergency fund. So where does the extra money come from?

There are many ways to earn extra money. Just remember that you have just set up your budget, and that should not change for a while. Extra money can come in the way of extra work, maybe part-time on time off from regular duties or overtime from your current job. However, do not be too strict here, for I do not want you to get discouraged at this point. For this process will work, just give it some time.

You will get pay increases. Be sure not to splurge too much with these. It is all right to celebrate this occasion, but do not go overboard. Celebrate, and then get back on track. In the beginning of your career, you may change jobs and be granted pay increases. This is great, but remember the budget process. Please stick to it. If you do find more money, please do not throw it away on things. Just get that emergency fund setup.

It may take a few months or a year to get this fund set up, but you can do it.

Do not spend any of the emergency fund money unless you really are desperate. You need to place this fund into a money market account. This account will pay a minimum dividend or interest, but it does pay more than just a simple checking account. If you do have to spend it, you must replace it ASAP. Then you can create your futures saving plan.

The budget is so important, and you must stick to it. Do not try to live beyond your means, ever. This is a no-no in financial planning. It is the number one lesson in life. If you understand and follow the rule not to spend more than you make, you are a giant step ahead of most people, even the ones who think that they are rich but have a lot of debt.

Early on, you need to set up a net worth spreadsheet. This is a spreadsheet that will let you know what you are worth now, and as we update this, it will tell you the savings and financial plan story. The net worth spreadsheet gives us the needed data to make some very educated moves with our money going forward.

On one side, list the total of each of your assets (cash, investments, home equity, and etc.) and the other side, list the total of each of your debts (home mortgage, auto loan, and etc.). The difference between these two totals is your net worth. In the beginning, you may be surprised. It may be negative or a have very small gain. That's all right, for we have work to do.

Just follow the plan. Update this spread sheet monthly. It will tell the story of where we are going. Some months it may go down, but our plan is to see this number become positive very quickly and began to grow by leaps and bounds!

At least now we have a plan that will let us know where we have been and where we are headed. Try it. It will now be fun to find ways to make this plan be very successful. It will be a lot more fun to see your net worth grow than it would be to have more things with a lot of debt. An important note here: do not borrow to just improve life to improve your lifestyle. Only use credit as the last resort. You are now in control.

Chapter 8: The Investment Setup

After you have a viable budget set up along with the net worth spreadsheet, you will need to seek ways to earn the most out of your savings. Do not place all of your money into a passbook savings account and expect it to grow into your retirement plan. The cost of living usually grows more than this passbook savings account; therefore, you will be going in the wrong direction.

Again, only place the emergency fund into the money market account. Continue to save into this account on a regular basis, but set a target amount for emergencies, and from time to time, take the excess funds, and move them into an account that will pay your more interest or dividends.

A Simplified Financial Retirement Plan

I like to think that I am somewhat conservative with my investments, so we will use my strategy for this "Simplified Financial Retirement Plan."

The next step is to place some money into a one year Certificate of Deposit (CD). You say, "Why put money into a CD account? This doesn't pay very much, anymore."

You are correct. It doesn't. This account, for the most part, pays only a little more than a money market account. The only thing is that the money market account is readily available, whereas, the CDs are locked into a specific time frame. You can get your money out if you need it for some emergency, but there will be a penalty for early withdrawal. This is just another conservative tool for our plan. We will never take much risk with our base. It will always be there. Then one can sleep better and not worry very much about our financial future. That's the plan – to be worry-free financially.

The CDs usually sell for as little as $500 or $1000 each, even though these only pay a little more than the money market account. Just do not get ahead of the game and invest everything into a high flying stock market account and try to get rich quick, or you probably will get burned and lose everything. If you do lose everything, it is not the end of the world; you just have to "bow up" and start over. This "Simplified Financial Retirement Plan" will work, if you follow it closely.

Stay very close to your plan and check it monthly to make sure everything is on track. I think you will see that you are headed in the right direction, quickly. Do not panic if something unusual happens, and your investment plans begins to move in the wrong direction. Just make sure that it is the market conditions causing the problem and not over spending causing the downturn. Whatever causes a downturn in your plan can be overcome. You just need to stay in tune with your plan, and your net worth spreadsheet will tell you the story from month to month. Just follow the plan!

After the first year of saving, you should be well on your way to riches; however, remember you are not there yet. We are just gaining steam. The plan would be, after the one-year CD matures, renew it for two years and buy another one for a year. Always roll over all of the dividend or interest so that you can get the compound effect. Now here we go. After the next year, when this second CD matures, renew it for three years and buy another CD for one year. Now you have three

CDs. You have one that will mature in one year, one for two years, and one for three years. That's called CD laddering. Each and every year, you will have a CD maturing, and each year now, you can just roll it over for three years of maturity. This way, you get more dividends for the longer term CD. Each of your three CDs will now be three years to maturity, but one will be maturing every year.

Now, if you want to, you can continue this process up to maybe five years of CD maturity, and you can earn even more. I only suggest three years for now because we have other things to discuss. Note that even though CDs normally do not pay much more than money market funds, we will still use this as another base layer to our plan. They will vary in payouts from time to time. You need to make certain that the Federal Government (FDIC) insures them.

Let's review! You now have a budget, a monthly net worth spreadsheet, an emergency fund, and three CDs with three years' maturity dates. Here we go. This sounds good. Doesn't it?

The only thing wrong with this plan at this point is that it doesn't pay us very much money. Therefore, "The Simplified Financial Retirement Plan" is certainly not complete. But it is a great accomplishment to get to this point so that one can feel good and be comfortable with the remainder of the plan.

Next, after you become comfortable with this plan, set up a second money market account. Remember the first money market account is for an emergency fund. This second one will be for other savings and investing for a little more risk later on. It pays only a little interest, but you have immediate access to your money. Save, save, and save into this account and watch it grow.

Review your budget and see if there are other ways to cut expenses without overdoing it. Remember, I do not want you to go without anything that you need and many things that you want. This plan does not include any pain and suffering. It must be fun. Just take a quick look to see what makes sense for you. You may be able to cut out some of the expenses for a short time, just to give your savings plan a much needed boost. Try it, and you will see that your net worth spreadsheet will tell you a very good story.

Live life to its fullest and have a lot of fun. Then, after the second money market account grows large enough, we need to buy a no-load mutual fund. I like the American Fund family. It is solid and has done well for me. There are many funds available. I also like the dividend growth and health sciences fund. Most of the time, there is a $2500 or $5000 minimum to purchase these funds. There will be a cost to buy and may be a small maintenance fee associated with these funds. However, do not fret, for you are now in the investment world and with this comes a cost.

So let's review. We have a budget that includes us living on 70% of our income and saving 30%. Consider this as a great accomplishment. However, this is only the beginning. By creating a good solid conservative foundation, we can now afford to take some risks.

Now let's take a look at the total savings. After this amount reaches a comfort zone, we then take 30% of the total savings and start to find ways to take some educated risk.

Remember we now have a small emergency fund, 3-years of laddered CDs, and the rest in a good mutual fund. That is a very good base or core for our master plan layout of our "Simplified Financial Retirement Plan," even though each of these investments only pays a very small interest or dividend. We will not get rich with this portion of our investment strategy. But hold on, there is more.

We then take the 30% of our savings and invest 20% into the total Standard and Poor's (S&P 500). The other 70% stays put. It stays fully invested as our financial base. The S&P 500 is an index fund, meaning that by owning this fund, you will own a portion of every stock that makes up this 500 stock index fund. What a deal!

My experience tells me that most money managers do not perform any better than the S&P 500 index fund over time. I know that some will tell you about their hot stocks that do perform very well, but look deeper into their managed portfolios, and the average will not beat the S&P 500 very many times. This fund has done well over the last few years, but no one knows what's ahead. It is just our best guess, so do not take undue risk with your hard-earned money. I would rather guess on the conservative side. I think it is a great idea to take this conservative approach to "The Simplified Financial Retirement Plan." Don't you? But we will take some risks later after we create this great financial base to our plan.

And by the way, the cost of purchasing shares of this fund can be small. Here's the best way to buy this fund and any other stocks. If you hire a financial consultant, it will be expensive because he will probably charge you a high fee each time you buy or sell a stock. If you hire a money manager, he will probably not charge for buying and selling stocks, he will just charge you a percentage based on your total portfolio. This can also be expensive. After all, he gets paid whether you make money or lose money. Of course, the more money in your portfolio, the more your manager gets paid, so it makes sense that he would do everything possible to make you more money. Therefore, if you need a professional, I do recommend the money manager. I have one. I will write more about this later in the book.

What about the other 10% of the savings?

We will invest this into the stock market. So here we go. This will certainly pose us a lot more risk, but let's look at ways to minimize our risk.

You may know by now that I am very high on dividends. So let's take a look at stocks that pay a dividend. To me, this is a no-brainer. The dividend stocks pay you whither the stocks go up or go down. Therefore, if the stock increases, you get a "double whammy". If the stock goes down, you still get paid the dividend.

This is my formula for buying stocks. First, the stock must pay a dividend. The stock needs to have a price to earnings (PE) ratio of less than 20. The (PE) ratio is calculated by dividing the stock price by the company's earnings per share for the previous year. It also must have a 50-day moving average above or trending upward toward the 200 moving average-day. Pay attention here. This is very important to my plan.

Once you get familiar with this, look at the stock, it will become an easy way to stay on track with buying and selling stock. I check this comparison weekly on each one of my stocks. I compare the 50-day moving average with the 200-day moving average. Once the stock starts to trend down toward this 200-day moving average, I pay a lot of attention to what is going on with it. If the 50-day moving average passes below this 200-day moving average, I sell, at least the principal. Then, I will not have any of my money at risk in this stock. I may sell it all, if something negative is going on with the company.

A note of caution: I usually do not do anything if the market falls suddenly for some apparent reason. I just hang in there until it rallies back and then continue with my plan. If you are ready for some real risk-taking, you can buy more of the stock at a low price, and as it comes back up, you will recoup your losses much sooner. It seems to always come back up over time. Remember, we don't have to be too concerned because we still have our really good base or core savings plan in place. Therefore, we can take some chances. Do not panic!!! The market will go up and down over time. Even the very best professional cannot time the ups and downs of the stock market.

The stocks that have done well for me are Deere, Ford, General Electric, Kraft Foods, Home Depot, and McDonalds. As I have stated, the past doesn't always prove to be great for the future, though. You have to look and study the current economic conditions before choosing the stock that fits your portfolio.

For the buying and selling of the stock portion of my plan, I use a discount broker. I can buy and sell, and also do a lot of free research with this discount broker. The cost of buying or selling through this discount broker is very small. You just have to be really careful and make sure to know what you are doing, for this process is very easy to screw up. It just takes the press of a computer button. I really tend to buy and hold my stocks as long as I can; however, the trends need to stay somewhat positive. After all, the more you buy and sell, the more cost that is incurred. You need to know what you are doing here. So be careful and good luck.

I review my stocks every week to see where each trend is headed. This is very simple and a fun way to invest. If I see one of my stocks begin a negative trend, I keep a close check on it. Remember, stocks only perform in your favor if you buy low and sell high. You have to be careful investing in the stock market, for the natural thing is to buy a stock that is hot and going higher. But usually by the time an amateur decides to buy this hot stock, it has lost it momentum, and after we buy, it peters out and goes down. Then, on the other hand, it is human nature that when we see one of our stocks go down, we want to sell it.

For the inexperienced investor, it is very difficult to invest into a falling stock market, but that is the formula to success in the market. One needs to have some cash available to invest when the stock market takes a dive. This is a very difficult task for a conservative investor.

This is why I like my plan to review each of my stocks using the 50-day moving average compared to the 200-day moving average. If one of my stocks trends or moves downward toward the 200-day average trend line as it crosses this 200-day trend line, I will sell it. Some call this crossing the "Golden Cross."

Do not worry about this. It is just the way the stock market works. After I sell my stock that moves below the 200-day average, I reinvest it into another stock that has a rising trend toward the 200-day average. I like to watch a stock and buy it just as it crosses above the "Golden Cross" 200-day trend line.

This way your profits go back up quicker than staying with the stock that you just sold with the downward trend line. You do not have to wait on the stock that you just sold to go back up again. After you sell it, you don't care where it goes. You are now invested in a new stock that is rising. You can also take the loss on your Federal income tax up to $3000 per year. Then, you will not have to declare the capital gains on your new stock that is rising until you sell it. This is called using the system to your benefit. Continue with this plan and move your money around in the market, as you need to get the very best profits.

You need to get somewhat educated with the stock market before taking a serious look into investing into it. I believe you need to learn how to take some controlled risks with only a small amount of money. Do what is best at time with the current circumstances. Be smart.

Remember, we are talking about averages here; therefore, it will take several days for the trend line to move very much, either up or down. This gives us some time to make some very calculated moves with our stocks.

I do not buy and hold when it comes to equity investments. When a stock sets a negative trend, I will sell and buy into a stock with a positive trend. This system has worked well for me.

I started my investing plan with $5000. I choose five good dividend-paying stocks that fit my plan, and I invested $1000 into each. In just a few years, this $5000 has grown to be a large part of my portfolio, just by following my plan. What a deal!

Remember, I do not invest any of my base money. It stays put. I know it does not pay a lot of interest, but I have it through thick and thin. This is my insurance policy for my total retirement plan. Of course, you can choose to take more risks than I do. Everyone needs to choose his or her own comfort level.

I have the 70% base with not much risk, 20% with some risks, and 10% with higher risks in the stock market. This set-up works best for me.

By using an online discount broker, this can be done without very much cost to you. This is a fun way to invest in the market, and it is easy. After all, remember the stock market investing is only a very small part of your portfolio. We have set up a very good base that will remain solid throughout this adventure.

You are living on 70% of your income, you have 30% going into savings, you have an emergency account fund set up in a money market account, you have at least 3-CDs, and you have a good solid mutual fund.

Then, you have 20% 0f the savings account money in the S&P 500 index fund, and you have the other 10% of the saving account invested in the stock market. What else could you want?

This is a very stable and diversified portfolio.

- Bulletproof your plan: There are a million ways to screw things up, but fortunately, just a few ways to get them right.
- Set financial goals, and track your process. Spend less than you earn, and save the difference.
- Pay as you go, and stay out of debt.
- Pay your mortgage off early and be a real homeowner.

- Remain calm during times of bad news and market volatility.
- Face money problems as they arise, get the facts, and take the appropriate action.
- Plan retirement well in advance, so you are prepared for "old age."

So do not worry yourself. All is good, and you will make it to a financially secure retirement. If the economy stays anywhere near normal (who knows what normal is these days?), we will be fine, financially by following this "Simplified Financial Retirement Plan."

Chapter 9: Death and Taxes

Someone has said that the only things in life that are certain are death and taxes. It takes a lot of money to live a good life, and it takes a lot of money to die.

We need to make sure we not only enjoy our life and money to its fullest, but also make sure that we have everything in place for our death. Our family does not need to have a burden placed on them at the time of our death.

You need a written will and a power of attorney. This needs to be done using a local attorney so that all of the legal aspect will be covered.

The written will covers who will get your money and other assets, and the power of attorney covers your desires if you become incapacitated. You will need a legal power of attorney for both financial and health aspects. The power of attorney will allow you to appoint a person to be in charge of your life and assets so that he or she can carry out your wishes, if you cannot.

You can get by without this process, but it makes everything go a whole lot smoother, and your wishes will not get tied up in probate court for a long period of time.

Long term care insurance is almost like a "Catch 22" situation. Long term care can be and is very expensive. If you get this insurance when you are young, it is less expensive, but you may pay the monthly premiums for many years, or if you wait until you are older to get this insurance, it is too expensive. Also, when you die, your heirs get nothing from this insurance.

 So, I say set aside an investment fund to cover a couple years of assisted living and also get a notarized statement saying that you do not want to remain on a life support system for a long period of time. Give your doctor a copy of this form for his files. Also, if you never use this investment fund, at least your heirs will get it.

Also, you need to take care of the last thing. That is funeral arrangements. If you want any special service or something of that nature, you need to meet with a funeral director so that he can help you set up your preferences. I say unless you have waited until you are retired or very old, just set up the services and do not pay in advance for it. It is much better to keep this money invested in the stock market so that it can grow larger for your heirs. They will tell you that the price of the funeral is rising all of the time, and this is true, but if this money is invested wisely, it will gain more than the cost of the funeral rises. Just make sure you have the total cost set aside so that your family can access it quickly to pay for the services. You do not want to place any undue burden on them during this time.

Chapter 10: Help is Available

Since I am now near retirement, I will be having some free time on my hands. Therefore, if you need help setting up your "Simplified Financial Retirement Plan," for a small fee, I will help you set up a budget so that you can live on 70% of your income.

If needed, I will also help you set up a net worth spreadsheet so that you can track your net worth monthly.

For a small percent of your investment gains, I will help you with your investments and track them for you on a monthly basis. I am cheap. I will only charge for your quarterly gains, and if you do lose anything, there will be no charge for that quarter. Now, where can you find a plan like that? Most financial helpers charge whether you gain or lose. Not me! I want each of you to be very

A Simplified Financial Retirement Plan

successful with this plan, and I will do everything in my power to make that happen with you.

You can contact me at johnnyfrye@sbcglobal.net, and we can set up a meeting to discuss it. There will be no charge for this initial meeting. I want to make sure you will enjoy this investment adventure.

I can also help you get set up with an attorney to help with the last will and testimony and the power of attorneys.

My advice for my readers:

- Make savings a regular part of living.
- Get started saving as early as you can. Live sensibly within your means.
- Start a regular savings plan, and think before you spend.
- Save regularly. Set a major goal that you want to achieve.
- Do not be afraid to set this goal very high. You can do it.
- Get into the habit of saving. Save anywhere. Just make sure you're saving something.
- Do not live beyond your means.
- Don't buy more of a house than you can afford.

- Be aware of your income vs. your expenses. Don't spend what you don't have.
- Learn more about money and how it works. Understand how to use money to your advantage.
- Learn to be a great negotiator.
- Plan for the long term.
- Take full advantage of a 401(k) and/or IRAs, and look for long-term returns.
- Don't forget about the bills that aren't monthly, like your insurance premiums, property taxes, and etc. Look at your bills for a year and set aside the money to pay for them.
- Start a monthly investment program with whatever money you can, as early in your life as you can.
- Plan on living to be 100 years old.
- Pay off your credit card every month if you can. Otherwise, at least make a serious dent in the balance.
- Learn the principle of compounding and take full advantage of it.
- Educate your kids on how to handle money. Get them involved early in life, and let them read this book!

Better yet, set yourself up on "The Simplified Financial Retirement Plan." It works. In my opinion, this is a well-diversified and conservative based plan that will lead you to a great, secure financial future.

I may be a little biased here, but it has been a lot of fun using trial and error to develop this plan that I have just shared with you. You can be successful with this plan, now that we have eliminated most of the error part.

Remember, start saving and investing as early as you can so that you can take full advantage of the power of compounding interest. I would like for you begin with a little more than $5/week savings as compared to today's dollars. This will allow you to get on track much quicker, considering all of the inflation that has occurred over the last several years. If you elect to start out very small, that's ok. The important thing is: just get started, and stay with the plan through thick and thin. It will work wonders for you. Try it! You may find out that you like it.

Set up a budget so that you can prioritize what is truly important to you, and adjust everything else to help you meet those goals. Certainly stay within your means. Work as long as it takes you to become financially secure, or as long as you're happy with your employment situation. Pay off credit cards each and every month.

The most important advice that I can give you is: Please don't spend what you do not have. Don't blow it because now you have a plan: "The Simplified Financial Retirement Plan."

By utilizing this plan, I have felt very good about retiring early, but as I have stated, I like to work, and I have a job that I enjoy very much. With my health still good, I will keep working for another few years. Who knows how much money is enough? There are a lot of unknowns out there.

However, I feel really good about my money management over the years. I never struck it rich or never had a family member leave me a large inheritance. I just made it on my own—from nothing to having a nice retirement plan in place. It does feel really good.

I could have lived well beyond my means by the way of credit, but I was way too conservative for that. I have had a very comfortable life over the years with a very supportive family to help me along life's pathway.

You now have the plan that I've used over the years. I learned from the ground up by educating myself using trial and error. Therefore, I had to move slowly and surely so as not to take too much risk. I was and still am fairly conservative.

I have worked very hard for my money, and I certainly want to make the most of it. I buy the things that I need and some of the things that I just want, just because I can. As you have read, I limit my risk with small investments.

I keep most of my money in some sort of conservative investment. Then, the more that I accumulate, the more I can branch out. But that doesn't mean that I just take a lot of uneducated risks. I just stay diversified in many areas of investments.

I like to think that I keep the odds in my favor most of the time. The real key is to start early. Save on a regular basis. Payroll deduction is the best, for you never have the money in your hands to spend. The decision has already been made.

I also think you need to make giving to the **Lord** automatic. After all, our Lord and Savior has given us life and everything that we have.

II Corinthians 9:7

Every man according as he purposeth in his heart, so let him give, not grudgingly, or of necessity: for God loveth a cheerful giver.

Malachi 3:10

Bring ye all the tithes into the storehouse, that there may be meat in mine house, and prove me now herewith, saith the Lord of hosts, if I will not open you the windows of heaven, and pour you out a blessing, that there shall not be room enough to receive it.

I firmly believe these scriptures; therefore the principles of "The Simplified Financial Retirement Plan" are based on this belief. We were born with no money, and we will not take it with us when we die. We will not need it in heaven.

Good luck! I look forward to helping any and all of my readers. Let's do it. It will be fun, and it will require very little effort or expense on your part. And remember "no gain", "no pay."

Don't make it complicated. I have laid out a very simple plan. I can help you. I will be there to help you understand the plan, and I will do all of the legwork involved in setting up the entire "Simplified Financial Retirement Plan."

After retirement sets in, we need take a look at life after the working years. I hope there are many years left so that we can now really enjoy and live out our plan. After all, it has taken us a lifetime of planning, saving, and investing to get here.

If you have followed "The Simplified Financial Retirement Plan," you should be able to retire in such a manner that you do not have to worry about money and can just live the good life. But, wait a minute! As we discussed earlier, you are already living the good life. Once you get set up with this great financial plan, you will want to keep going. It is fun.

Now that you are retired, rework your budget with those retirement costs, for they will now change a little. I can help with this if needed, for I have done a lot of homework on this plan.

You have full Social Security checks coming in. If you continue to work for a few more years because you want to, then you will elect to sign up for "Part A" of Medicare. This is hospitalization insurance. It is free. Free is good, even though I always tell my wife to be aware that nothing is really free. Everything comes with a price. I certainly have found this statement to be true over the years.

After you quit working and no longer have any medical insurance, you will need to sign up for "Part B" of Medicare. It is not free. It now costs a little over a hundred dollars a month. Not to worry! you have the money because this will become a new budget item.

This Medicare "Part B" will cover 80% of the medical costs. You will be responsible for the other 20%. So you will now need to get a separate supplementary insurance policy. There are many available. So review your needs, and pick the best policy suited for you. Good luck with that. Again, the cost for most of these policies is maybe a couple hundred dollars a month.

While you are young, you will need some life insurance to help your family make ends meet, financially, if you should pass away. I recommend term life insurance. Most employers will cover your salary for free, and the next level is usually fairly cheap. So go for two times your salary. Then, after you retire, there should be no need for this expense. If you have followed "The Simplified Financial Retirement Plan," you will be fine.

Once you rework your budget for your retirement needs, there will be enough money to make you happy and secure with your retirement. Now it is time to spend some of that hard-earned, saved, and invested money.

Not so fast. I think one needs to be very wise, as we have now learned that life is not all that simple. Things happen, and we still need to be prepared for the unexpected. So continue to follow a good balanced budget, retain the emergency fund, and continue to manage your investments. It can still be fun.

Your budget income will be any retirement fund that you may have been lucky enough to retain from your working years, Social Security, and money from your retirement plan. If you have followed "The Simplified Financial Retirement Plan," you will not need to touch any of these funds. But you may want to withdraw only about 4% monthly from this fund. Therefore, the interest and the dividends from this account will be greater than 4% annually, and your net worth will still be growing. What a deal! See, I told you this is a great plan. Don't you agree?

I certainly hope you have a 401(k) plan or an IRA account, and if you do, you will have to draw some of that money out of the plan the year after you turn 70-and-a-half. The taxes will need to be paid on the money that you have to withdraw from this account. I think they decided the amount that you must draw out annually by saying that you should live on average of 18 more years; therefore, your total is divided by 18, and that is the amount that you must withdraw and pay federal taxes on annually.

Set up your retirement budget accordingly, and you will be fine. Only use the retirement savings fund to purchase large ticket items such as an automobile, travel, and fun stuff. After all, you earned it by using a very smart "Simplified Financial Retirement Plan." By now, you know how to spend your money wisely, so have fun in those retirement years, and be worry-free from any monetary issues. Remember, we are planning on living to be 100 years old, and then we will weigh our options. Our plan also includes an early retirement, if we want it. After all, we can now be in control of our finances. For, by following this plan, our goal, is to someday to have more than a million dollars of equity and a couple million dollars of net worth. Now, how about this plan? It sounds too good to be true, but it is possible. Why not try it?

I do not believe you can reach this goal by saving only. You will need some very unique investing ideas, some of which we have covered in this book. But remember, do not dwell on the past market conditions. You have to look at the trends going forward. Start early and use the compound interest technique. You will be surprised how this process will help your portfolio grow by leaps and bounds over the years. The more you have, the larger and faster it will grow.

One last thing: just think what would happen if we started teaching our kids about money in school when they are still young enough to make a real difference in their lives.

Just think of three kinds of people who go to McDonald's, play video games, and have cell phones. Some of these people eat there, play games with it, and others own it. We need to have our goals set to own the place. Set your goals high early in life. You will be glad you did. Always treat others better than they expect you to treat them. Also, in closing, you may want to begin your plan with saving a little. This worked for me early on, but you need to compare your savings' dollar to today's economy.

Chapter 11: Summary

We seem to have several phases in our lives. I believe that we must live each separate phase as its own as we plan for the next one to come.

In the beginning when we are born, we have relatively no concerns. All we have to do is be the baby, but we soon discover that life is filled with changes.

We grow up and learn that life is very full of surprises. We soon find out that we need to plan for the unknown changes or different phases of our lives. We certainly don't need to be like many who kind of stick their heads in the sand and think that all will be fine, and everything will work itself out. However, to be truthful, most things will work themselves out. But they will not always work out for the best for each of us.

We must learn early on to plan ahead. This gives us some control over much of our future. We never get to stay in any phase of our lives very long. Also, I have found that after you get somewhat older, the phases comes a lot more quickly. So we must be prepared. I know that many times we would prefer to remain the same for a long period of time, but that is not how life works. About the time we get a little complacent, here comes another change. We must learn how to move from one phase of our lives to the next without question or trying to hold on to the past. The past is the past, and it makes great memories, for the most part. One needs to be looking forward to the very exciting things that are beginning to take shape in the next phase of our lives.

We are born to live and die and present ourselves as a testimony for our Lord and Savior who allowed us to be present in this world in the first place.

As we look back over our lives, we can remember that some of our most rewarding years were spent learning new ways to live our lives. Most of these experiences came from our peers and learning for ourselves by trial and error.

Therefore, it is the best-case scenario, going forward, to review our peers and seek out who will supposedly have the best chance of leading us in a very positive direction. I have found that being around positive people has a very good effect on my life. It helps me to have a much better attitude and not see the world as a place that is falling apart around me. This, in turn, helps me with my every day decision-making.

Retirement is my next phase. I hope I am prepared. Talking with others, it seems that this can be an exciting phase of life. Many have retired early and gone back to work, either part-time or full-time, doing something that they really enjoy. If you have a very stressful job during your working years, it would be the right thing to retire early and make the best of your retirement years, but for me, I have enjoyed working in the paper bag industry for more than 50 years, and I have delayed retirement until late in life. I wouldn't have it any other way.

The key to a successful retirement seems to be that one needs to stay busy. Do not just sit and fade away. Stay active as long as you can, and interact with friends and family often. And take that medicine. I think there is a pill for almost anything these days.

And by the way, now that you have made headway into "The Simplified Financial Retirement Plan," You can spend some of that hard earned and wisely invested retirement CASH!!! Just stay in touch with the PLAN, and you should be just fine.

We need to remember to keep it simple. It is not all about money. It is about life. Everything is intertwined. Everything is connected. Our lives. Our money. Our . . . everything.

I must remind you first, that we should never forget the value of life, and second, do something with it. It's why I like to put everything in perspective. The good things along with the bad shape us into the people we will become.

I hope you have enjoyed this book as much as I have enjoyed writing it. Thank you for reading it. Maybe something that I wrote will help you along life's highway. May God Bless you.

John Frye